Martin Weber

A Map of Latin American Dreams

January 12–March 5, 2004
Reception: February 26, 6–8 PM

Light Work

ROBERT B. MENSCHEL MEDIA CENTER
316 Waverly Avenue, Syracuse New York 13244

Gallery hours are 10 AM to 6 PM Sunday through Friday except for school holidays

"Dreams are real. They exist," states Martin Weber. In the series *A Map of Latin American Dreams*, Weber aspires to record the hopes and dreams of his subjects, and to assemble an archive of portraits created throughout Latin America.

In the sixties, Weber's parents emigrated from Argentina to Chile, where he was born in 1968, and then returned to Buenos Aires in 1974. He was raised in an atmosphere of democratic instability that left its imprint in Latin America, where military coups applied fear and censorship to freedom of speech and ideas. Weber feels that "Latin America is a land of contradictions and broken dreams. A place where countries are being rebuilt again and again almost every ten years." As the title of the series implies, Weber's intention is to draft his own map of Latin America, not of geographic boundaries or variations of terrain, but of the fragile landscape in which everyday reality lives together with secrets and dreams, reflecting on personal and historical contexts.

Weber has photographed in Argentina, Cuba, Nicaragua, Peru, and along the US-Mexican border. For this series, he asked his subjects to imagine what they desired most and instructed them to inscribe it on a small chalkboard. His subjects assumed an active role in their portrayals by choosing what to reveal. In the act of creating this work, Weber facilitates an intimate exchange between the subject and viewer, as if each subject is disclosing a secret for the viewer to take in.

Weber looked back to his early studies in acting and theater while creating this work. The exaggerated theatrical appearance of many of his subjects parallels the instruction that stage actors are given to project their gestures and expressions for the benefit of the audience seated in the back rows of a theater. Whether working with a single individual or an ensemble cast, each photograph is carefully staged by Weber. Every subject's position and expression denotes a specific relationship to their surroundings, or to the other individuals present in the frame.

Expanding the notion of the photographic portrait, Weber creates a multifaceted tableau vivant in which he actively directs the principle characters and settings. Weber's participation also allows his subjects the potential to gain control over their own

"Los sueños son reales. Existen," afirma Martín Weber. En la serie *Un Mapa de Sueños Latinoamericanos*, Weber aspira a registrar las esperanzas y sueños de sus sujetos y componer un archivo de retratos creados a lo largo de Latinoamérica.

A fines de los sesenta, sus padres emigraron de Argentina a Santiago de Chile donde nació en 1968, luego se radicaron nuevamente en Buenos Aires en 1974. Se crió en una atmósfera de inestabilidad democrática que marcaron a Latinoamérica, en donde los golpes militares aplicaron el miedo y la censura a la libertad de expresión. Weber siente que "Latinoamérica es una tierra de contradicciones y sueños rotos. Un lugar donde países son reconstruidos una y otra vez casi cada diez años." Como el título de esta serie lo indica, su intención es bosquejar su propio mapa de Latinoamérica, uno que no muestra los límites geográficos o variaciones en el terreno, sino que busca explorar el terreno frágil en el que la realidad cotidiana convive con secretos y sueños, reflejando contextos históricos y personales.

Hasta ahora Weber ha fotografiado en Argentina, Cuba, Nicaragua, Perú y a lo largo de la frontera de México y Estados Unidos. Para esta serie, él les solicita a sus sujetos que se imaginen lo que mas desean y les pide que lo escriban en un pequeño pizarrón. Así, asumen un rol activo en los retratos al elegir qué revelar. En el acto de crear su obra, Weber facilita un íntimo intercambio entre el sujeto y el espectador, como si cada uno revelara un secreto para que el espectador lo tome.

Weber se refirió a sus estudios de actuación y teoría teatral mientras creaba esta obra. La apariencia teatral de muchos de sus sujetos tienen un paralelo con las instrucciones que los actores de escena reciben para proyectar sus gestos y expresiones para el beneficio de la audiencia sentada en las últimas filas del teatro. Asimismo, cuando trabaja con un individuo o con un grupo, cada fotografía es cuidadosamente dirigida por Weber, cada posición y expresión de los sujetos denotan una relación específica con su entorno, o con los otros individuos presentes en el cuadro.

Expandiendo la noción del retrato fotográfico, crea un multifacético tableu vivant en el cual dirige activamente las puestas en escena y sujetos principales y a la vez crea el espacio donde los retratados retienen

representation. The personal expressions that Weber makes possible for his subjects range from the specific to the universal. Some wish for "Lots of horses," or long to "Marry an American." Others dream of a bigger picture where "You never feel alone," or simply express a wish "To have friends." If these quotes were separated from the images, we could imagine some of the same dreams coming from our own friends, families, or co-workers. Sobering wishes such as, "My wish is to find the body of my son, fallen in combat against Samoza's dictatorship and give him a proper burial," add a raw reality to the framework of the project.

The photographs in this body of work allow the individuals represented to express their dreams, and through the presentation of these images in exhibitions and publications, Weber extends that opportunity to a much wider audience. The exhibition is currently on display at Light Work's main gallery. Already several comments that are jotted down in the gallery's visitor book such as, "Thank you for reminding me of a world that exists outside of my very narrow sheltered one," and "I hope someday my images will be as inspiring as these—I take my life for granted too much," could be included in photographs yet unmade.

The people of Latin America represent a complex cultural and political mosaic shaped by Indigenous peoples, early European explorers and conquerors, African slaves, numerous European currents of immigration, and several hundred years of political change and unrest. By focusing his camera on the dreams and aspirations of individuals, Weber is able to distinguish the most essential detail of a much larger map. For Weber, this "map of Latin American dreams" could take a lifetime to complete, but through this work he acknowledges and celebrates the enduring human spirit that allows one to dream, even in the most difficult circumstances.

Gary Hesse
Associate Director
Light Work

poder sobre su representacíon. Las expresiones personales de los sujetos oscilan entre lo muy específico a lo universal. Algunos desean "Muchos caballos," o anhelan "Casarme con un Yuma." Otros sueñan con un cuadro más ámplio donde "Que nunca te sientas sola," o simplemente expresan un deseo "Tener amigos." Si estas citas estuvieran separadas de las imágenes, podríamos imaginarnos algunos de los mismos deseos viniendo de nuestros propios amigos, familias, o compañeros de trabajo. Luego, deseos como "Encontrar el cuerpo de mi hijo caído durante la dictadura de Somoza y darle sana sepultura," nos devuelven y despiertan a una realidad cruda que encuadra el proyecto.

Las fotografías en este trabajo permiten a los individuos representados expresar sus sueños, y a través de la presentación de estas imágenes en exhibiciones y publicaciones, Weber extiende esa oportunidad a una audiencia aún más ámplia. La muestra se encuentra actualmente en exhibición en la galería principal de Lightwork. Ya varios comentarios que están apuntados en el libro de visitas de la galería como, "Gracias por recordarme acerca de un mundo que existe más allá del mío, estrecho y protegido" y "Espero algun día mis imágines sean tan inspiradoras como éstas—doy por supuesta demasiado de mi vida" pudieran ser incluídas en imágines todavía no hechas.

La gente de Latinoamérica representa un complejo mosaico cultural y político formado por los pueblos indígenas, los primeros exploradores europeos y conquistadores, esclavos africanos, varias corrientes inmigratorias europeas y varios cientos de años de cambios políticos y desasosiego. Al enfocar su cámara en los sueños y aspiraciones de individuos, Weber logra distinguir en detalle lo escencial de un mapa más ámplio. Para él, este "mapa de sueños Latinoaméricanos" puede tomar una vida para completar pero, a través de este trabajo, da cuenta y celebra el perdurable espíritu humano que nos permite a cada uno soñar, aún en las circunstancias más difíciles.

Gary Hesse
El Director Asociado
Light Work

Work for my family, Seclantas, Argentina

Lots of horses, Los Conquistadores, Argentina

That my mother lives 50 years more, San Antonio de Areco, Argentina

I wish to acquire a business and a vehicle to live better, Casabindo, Argentina

That we have good health, lots of love, friendship, and peace from God, Misiones, Argentina

To be a lawyer, La Niña, Argentina

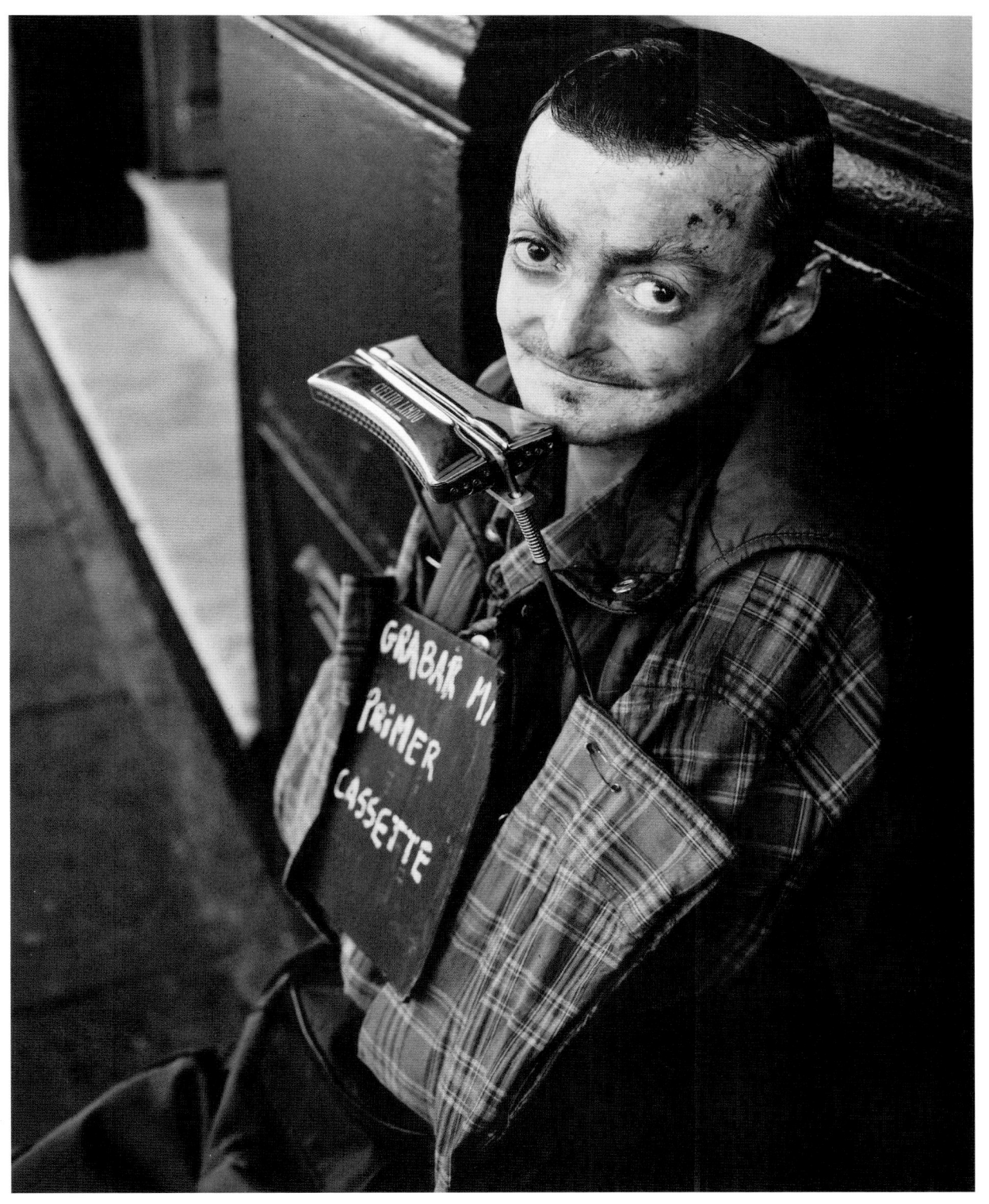

To record my first cassette, Buenos Aires, Argentina

To marry an American, La Habana, Cuba

I wish to be a child again, La Habana, Cuba

One glove for each—4 lefties—5 righties, La Habana, Cuba

I wish to be a poet, La Habana, Cuba

To have happiness to have, to be able to live, La Habana, Cuba

I have the wish that everybody lives well so I can be happy, Seclanias, Argentina

That our needs don't disturb our dreams, La Habana, Cuba

I want to be a policewoman, Maclovio Rojas, Mexico-USA border

That you never feel alone, Oaxaca, Mexico

My biggest wish is to finish my studies, Maclovio Rojas, Tijuana, Mexico

That my mother comes, Orphanage, Maclovio Rojas, Mexico-USA border

Affection, Maclovio Rojas, Mexico-USA border

I want to go to Puerto Rico, Imperial Beach, USA

My dream is that my daughter gets married, San Diego, USA

To have more clients to cure, so I can maintain my family, Ollantaytambo, Peru

To be a tourist guide, Cuzco, Peru

We want to knit blankets, we want photograph, and to sell the alpaca blankets, and I will spin them, Pizac, Peru

To find the way to express what I carry inside, Cuzco, Peru

I want my house to be big and fenced in, Chinchero, Peru

To come out of the crisis and have something for tomorrow, Cuzco, Peru

A long life with no sadness, Ollantaytambo, Peru

Peace in the world—Social justice in the world—Peace with God—To win the lottery, Cuzco, Peru

My dream is to meet people who will help me leave the place I am in and travel, Lima, Peru

My wish is to find the body of my son, fallen in combat against Somoza's dictatorship, and give him a proper burial, Esteli, Nicaragua

To leave poverty behind, Leon, Nicaragua

Return to Europe, Granada, Nicaragua

To have enough money to have a child, Altagracia, Nicaragua

To have a Nintendo, Granada, Nicaragua

To have a home and a dignified life, Matagalpa, Nicaragua

To have friends, Matagalpa, Nicaragua

My wish is to see my sons prepared to face the problems of unemployment, Granada, Nicaragua

That my son sends me what he promised, the money, Granada, Nicaragua

Death to imperialism and all forms of exploitation, Leon, Nicaragua